67 FUN & FASCINATING FACTS FOR KIDS

ANIMALS, PLANETS, DINOSAURS, WEIRD SCIENCE & COOL TRIVIA CHALLENGES

THIS BOOK BELONGS TO:

Published by
GRAPEVINE BOOKS

www.grapevinebooks.com
email: contact@grapevinebooks.com

Ordering Information:
Quantity sales: Special discounts are available on quantity purchases by corporations, associations, and others. For details, reach out to the publisher.

First published by Grapevine Books 2025

Welcome to The World of 6-7

What if a single number could unlock dozens of strange, exciting, and surprising facts about the world around you?

This book is built around the number 67, a number that keeps appearing in unexpected places. It shows up in the animal kingdom, in outer space, deep in Earth's history, and even in everyday science you might not notice at first. Each page reveals one fascinating idea, all connected by that same number, but never in the same way twice.

Inside these pages, you will discover animals that climb walls, dive through the air, call out through the night, and work together in ways that almost feel impossible. You will meet dinosaurs that survived by staying still, hiding underground, guarding nests, or relying on armor instead of speed. You will travel to planets where gravity feels heavier, storms last longer, and time does not behave the way it does on Earth. You will also uncover weird science hiding in sound, light, motion, and energy, showing that the ordinary world is far stranger than it seems.

Each fact is designed to be easy to read but full of meaning. You do not need to be a science expert to enjoy this book. You can open to any page, read one fact, and walk away knowing something new. Some facts explain how animals survive. Others reveal how scientists figure things out using clues left behind in fossils, light, or movement. A few might even change how you see things you thought you already understood.

This is not a book you have to read from beginning to end. You can flip around, jump between sections, or challenge yourself to notice how the number 67 connects ideas across animals, planets, dinosaurs, and science. You might spot patterns. You might ask questions. You might even want to dig deeper and learn more on your own.

Science is not just about answers. It is about curiosity, observation, and noticing details that others might miss. This book invites you to do exactly that, using one surprising number as your guide.

Get ready to explore 67 fun and fascinating facts, and discover how one number can open up an entire world of wonder.

Before You Dive In

This book is all about exploring, not memorizing. You do not need to read it from the first page to the last page. You can jump around, skip sections, or open to any fact that catches your eye.

Each page is connected by the number 67, but the facts themselves are very different. Some explain how animals survive. Others explore planets, dinosaurs, or strange science hiding in everyday things. The drawings are meant to help you see the idea, not explain everything in words. Take a moment to look closely before you read.

You might notice that some facts are short and some are longer. That is on purpose. Some ideas are quick surprises, while others need a little more time to sink in. If something makes you curious, pause and think about it. If something confuses you, that is okay too. Curiosity often starts with confusion.

There are no trick questions here and no right way to read this book. Wonder, imagination, and questions are encouraged. If one fact sends you looking up more information, that is a win.

Now turn the page, pick a fact, and dive in.

WEIRD SCIENCE

MEET THE MAGNET MASTER: ELEMENT 67

Element number 67 is called **holmium**, and every single holmium atom contains exactly **67 protons.**

Holmium might not be as famous as gold or iron, but it is a quiet powerhouse. It has one of the strongest magnetic strengths of any natural element, which makes it useful in special magnets, lasers, and some medical equipment.

Scientists use holmium in technology that needs precise control and strong magnetic force. That single number, 67, is what defines holmium's identity and gives it its unique properties, proving that even a tiny number can unlock big scientific power.

YOUR BODY HAS A 67-DAY BUILDING PLAN

Some human tissues, like parts of the skin and connective tissue, can take around 67 days to fully regenerate.

This means your body is **constantly rebuilding itself**, even when you are not aware of it. Cells divide, repair damage, and replace old cells on a schedule that can last weeks. The number 67 shows how patient and organized the human body really is.

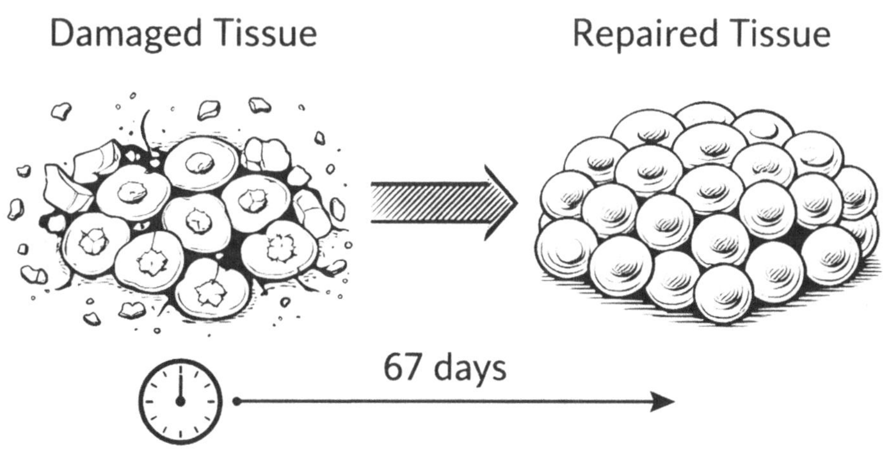

A SOUND THAT LASTS 67 SECONDS CAN FEEL LONGER

Studies show that a continuous sound lasting about 67 seconds can start to feel **much longer** to the human brain.

Your brain does not measure time like a clock. Instead, it judges time based on attention, boredom, and change. When a sound does not change, your brain stretches the experience, making 67 seconds feel strangely endless.

THE BRAIN CAN FIRE 67 SIGNALS IN A BLINK

In certain situations, a single neuron can send up to 67 electrical signals per second.

These rapid signals help your brain react quickly to danger, movement, and sound. Even though each signal is tiny, together they allow you to think, move, and feel in real time.

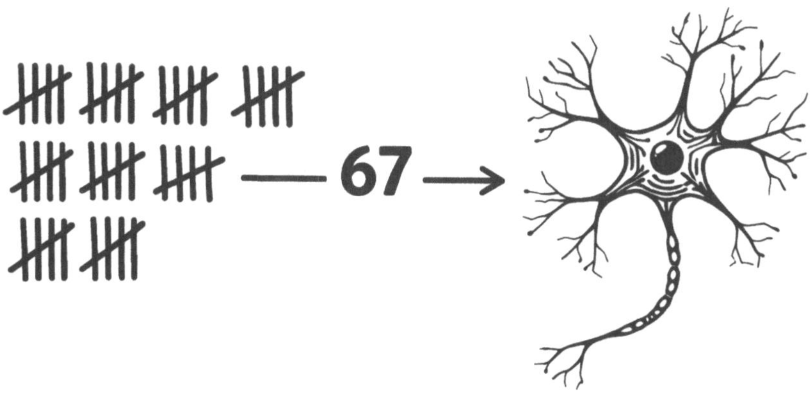

A 67-DAY ORBIT EXISTS IN OUR SOLAR NEIGHBORHOOD

When you walk from bright sunlight into a dark room, your eyes can take around 67 seconds to begin adjusting to the darkness.

At first, everything looks black because the light-sensitive cells in your eyes are overwhelmed by brightness. Inside your retina are special cells called rods that help you see in low light. These rods slowly become more sensitive as a chemical inside them, called rhodopsin, rebuilds itself. This process cannot be rushed.

As the seconds pass, your pupils widen to let in more light, and your brain starts to process shadows instead of sharp details. After about a minute, you can begin to notice shapes, movement, and outlines. Full night vision can take much longer, but that first 67 seconds is when your eyes switch from day mode to night mode.

THE 67-DEGREE TRICK BEHIND EVERY RAINBOW

Rainbows form when light bends, reflects, and spreads out inside water droplets, and one key angle involved is **about 67 degrees**.

When sunlight enters a raindrop, it slows down and bends. Inside the drop, the light reflects off the back surface and bends again as it exits. The angle at which this happens determines where the rainbow appears in the sky. Around 67 degrees, the colors separate clearly enough for our eyes to see them as **a curved band**. This is why rainbows always appear at a certain position relative to the Sun and the viewer. The rainbow is not actually “out there” in one spot, but created by light hitting droplets at just the right angle.

67 MILLION SPARKS IN A BLINK

A small static shock can involve **around 67 million tiny electrical sparks**, all happening in an instant.

When you walk across a carpet, electrons build up on your body. Touching metal suddenly releases that energy. Instead of one big spark, the discharge happens as millions of microscopic sparks jumping across the gap. **Each spark is too small to see** on its own, but together they create the shock you feel. Scientists study static electricity to protect electronics and understand how lightning forms on a much larger scale.

67 MINUTES BEFORE THE BRAIN STARTS DAYDREAMING

During quiet or repetitive activities, the human brain often begins drifting into daydream mode after **about 67 minutes**.

When there is little new information to process, the brain slowly reduces its focus on the outside world. Instead of staying alert, it switches to what scientists call the "**default mode**," where thoughts begin to wander. Memories, ideas, and imaginary scenes start to appear without effort. This is **not a mistake** or a failure of focus. It is actually how the brain rests and reorganizes itself.

Scientists believe this mental drifting helps with creativity and problem-solving. It allows the brain to connect ideas in new ways and review information from earlier experiences. That is why ideas often pop into your head when you are bored, relaxed, or doing something simple. After about 67 minutes of low stimulation, the brain quietly shifts gears, turning downtime into thinking time.

WHY 67 PERCENT BATTERY CHARGE FEELS FAST

When you plug in a device, the battery often charges quickly at first and then slows down after it reaches **around 67 percent**.

This happens because batteries are designed to fill up in stages. At lower levels, electricity can flow in freely, so the battery "**races**" upward. As the battery fills, it becomes more sensitive to heat and pressure. To protect it, the charging system slows things down. This prevents overheating and helps the battery last longer over time.

Engineers design chargers this way on purpose. Even though it feels like the battery is **suddenly getting lazy after 67 percent**, it is actually being careful. That fast climb at the beginning is for speed, and the slower finish is for safety and battery health.

WHEN WATER GETS BUSY AT 67 DEGREES

Water may look calm, but at **around 67 degrees Fahrenheit**, it quietly starts acting differently.

At this temperature, water molecules gain just enough energy to move more freely across the surface. They begin slipping away into the air faster, even though the **water does not feel warm** to the touch. This is why puddles shrink more quickly on mild days and why damp towels dry faster indoors than in cool rooms. Scientists pay close attention to this range because it marks a shift between slow, sleepy water and more active water. At 67 degrees, water is not boiling or freezing, but it is definitely on the move.

THE WOBBLE ZONE AT 67 PERCENT FULL

A container that is **about 67 percent full** is often harder to carry than one that is nearly empty or completely full.

When a container is partly filled, the contents inside can slide and slosh around. As you lift it, the weight shifts suddenly, pulling your arms in different directions. Your muscles have to work harder to stay balanced, even if the **container is not very heavy**. When a container is full, the contents cannot move as much, so it feels more stable. Engineers study this effect when designing fuel tanks, water bottles, and backpacks, because controlling moving weight is much harder than carrying steady weight.

ANIMALS

67 POUNDS OF SWEET GOLD

A healthy beehive can produce **up to 67 pounds of honey** in a single year.

Worker bees spend their days flying from flower to flower, collecting nectar and bringing it back to the hive. Inside the hive, the nectar is passed between bees, slowly thickening into honey. This honey is stored as food for the colony, especially during winter when flowers disappear. Producing 67 pounds of honey takes thousands of trips and teamwork from tens of thousands of bees, making honey one of nature's most organized group efforts.

THE ONE-LEG TRICK POWERED BY 67 PERCENT STRENGTH

A **flamingo** uses about **67 percent** of its leg strength when standing on just one leg.

What looks like a balancing act is actually a smart energy-saving move. Flamingos have special joints that allow their leg to lock into place, so they do not need to constantly use muscles to stay upright. Standing on one leg also helps **reduce heat loss** when the bird is in cold water. The raised leg is tucked close to the body to stay warm. Flamingos often switch legs while resting to stay comfortable. Using 67 percent of their strength efficiently allows them to rest without sitting down. This clever posture lets flamingos relax while staying alert.

67 JUMPING COUSINS

There are about **67 different species** in the kangaroo family, including kangaroos, wallabies, wallaroos, and tree kangaroos.

All of these animals belong to a group called macropods, which means **"big foot."** While they all move by hopping, they live in very different environments. Some race across open plains, some climb rocky hills, and others live in forest trees. Even though they share strong tails and powerful legs, each of the 67 species has adapted to survive in its own unique way.

THE 67 MUSCLES BEHIND A GIRAFFE'S NECK

A **giraffe's neck** may look simple, but it is controlled by **around 67 muscles** working together every moment of the day.

These muscles allow the giraffe to do many difficult things with ease. They help lift the head high into trees to reach leaves other animals cannot. They also guide the head slowly down to the ground to drink water, a position that requires careful balance and strength. When male giraffes fight, they swing their long necks with surprising force, using those same muscles to control movement and power. Even when a giraffe is standing still, its neck muscles stay active to keep the head steady. Supporting such a long neck is a full-time job, and those 67 muscles make sure the giraffe can eat, move, and stay upright without tipping over.

67 WINGS IN ONE FAMILY

The **hummingbird** family includes **about 67 major groups** of closely related species.

Hummingbirds are known for their tiny size and fast wingbeats. Their wings can beat dozens of times per second, allowing them to hover in midair while feeding on nectar. Across these 67 groups, hummingbirds show a huge variety of colors, beak shapes, and flight styles, all adapted to different flowers and habitats. Despite their size, they are some of the most specialized birds on Earth.

67 BONES IN A POWERFUL FLIPPER

Some large marine mammals, such as certain **whales** and **dolphins**, have **around 67 bones** in a single flipper.

These flippers may look simple from the outside, but inside they are packed with bones arranged like a hand with fingers. This structure allows whales to steer, turn, and balance as they swim through the ocean. The number of bones helps create strength and flexibility at the same time, which is essential for life in water.

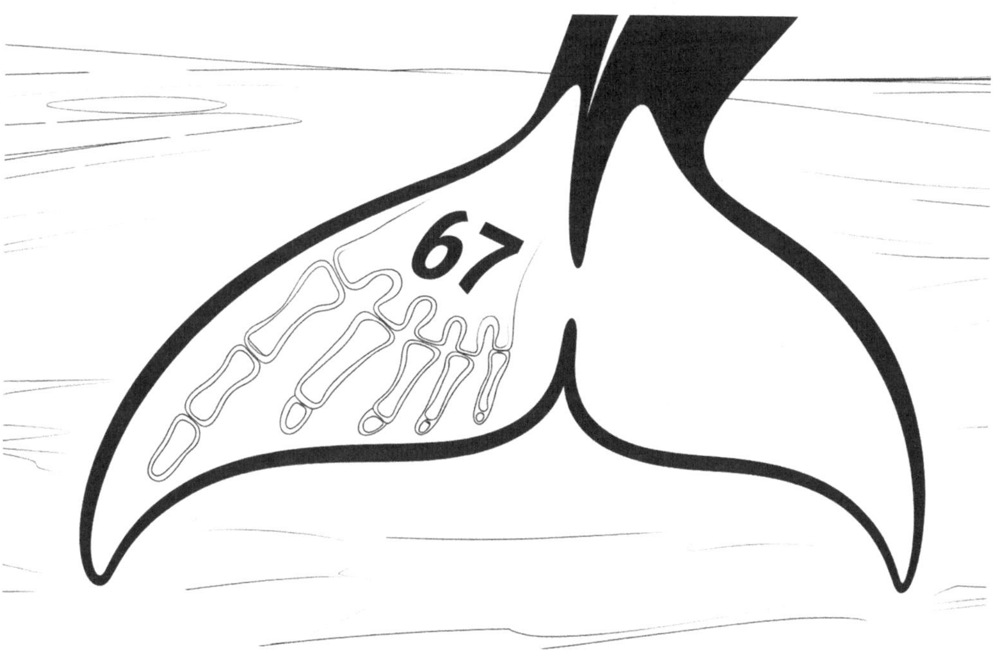

67 DAYS TO GROW FEATHERS

In some **bird species**, it can take **about 67 days** for young birds to fully grow their flight feathers.

During this time, chicks rely on their parents for food and protection. As the feathers grow longer and stronger, the birds practice flapping and balancing. By the end of this period, their wings are ready for flight, marking a major step toward independence.

67 MILES WITHOUT A STOP

Some migratory birds are capable of flying **up to 67 miles** in one continuous stretch without landing.

Before these long flights, birds carefully prepare by eating extra food and storing it as fat. This stored energy fuels their muscles while they fly for hours at a time. During migration, stopping in the wrong place can be dangerous due to predators, bad weather, or lack of food. Flying nonstop for long distances helps these birds cross open water, deserts, and other risky areas safely. Their ability to **travel 67 miles** or more without resting shows how precisely their bodies are adapted for long journeys.

DIVING LIKE A MISSILE AT 67 METERS PER SECOND

A **peregrine falcon** can dive at speeds close to **67 meters per second** when hunting.

During a dive, the **falcon folds its wings and drops** from high above its prey. Air rushes past as the bird accelerates downward with incredible precision. Special feathers and nostrils help control airflow and protect the lungs. Sharp eyesight guides the falcon straight to its target. This diving speed makes the peregrine falcon one of the fastest animals on the planet. That 67-meter-per-second plunge is a perfectly controlled attack.

67 TEETH IN A SHARK'S LIFETIME

Over the course of its life, a shark can grow and replace **around 67 sets of teeth.**

Shark teeth are designed to fall out easily, which may seem strange at first. When a tooth breaks or wears down, another one moves forward to take its place. This process happens continuously, ensuring the shark always has sharp teeth for hunting. Some sharks may go through thousands of individual teeth in their lifetime, but those teeth are **organized into repeated sets.** This system allows sharks to stay effective hunters for decades.

HEARING HIGH SOUNDS UP TO 67 KILOHERTZ

A dolphin can hear and produce sounds reaching **around 67 kilohertz**, far beyond human hearing.

These high-frequency sounds are used for echolocation, a system that helps dolphins "**see**" with sound. Dolphins send out rapid clicks and listen for echoes bouncing back from objects. From these echoes, they can tell **how far away** something is, **how big** it is, and even **what shape** it has. This ability helps them hunt fish, avoid obstacles, and navigate murky water. Even in total darkness, sound creates a clear picture of the world. Hearing up to 67 kilohertz turns the ocean into a detailed map.

67 CALLS IN ONE NIGHT

During breeding season, some **frogs** can produce **up to 67 calls** in a single night.

These calls are used to **attract mates and to signal territory** to other frogs. Each call requires energy, and frogs must balance calling with resting to avoid exhaustion. In warm, wet conditions, ponds and wetlands can fill with overlapping frog calls, creating a loud nighttime chorus. Reaching 67 calls in one night shows how important communication is for frog survival and reproduction.

67 STRIPES TO STAY SAFE

Some **zebras** have **around 67 visible stripes** across their bodies.

The stripe pattern does more than create a striking appearance. Scientists believe the stripes help **confuse predators** when zebras move together in groups. The patterns may also help regulate body temperature by affecting how heat moves across the skin. Because each zebra's stripes are unique, they also help individuals recognize one another within a herd.

67 STEPS TO SURVIVAL

A **spider's web** may look delicate, but building it is a careful process that can involve **up to 67 separate attachment points.**

As the spider moves, it fastens silk strands to leaves, branches, walls, or rocks, creating many anchor points that hold the web in place. Each attachment helps spread out the force when an insect hits the web at high speed. By planning where every strand goes, the spider creates a structure that bends without breaking. The more attachment points a web has, the stronger it becomes, giving the spider a better chance of catching food and staying alive.

CLIMBING ANYWHERE WITH 67 STICKY GRIP PADS

A **gecko** can climb walls and ceilings using **around 67 rows of sticky pads** on its toes.

Each toe is covered with flat pads lined in neat rows, and each row holds millions of microscopic hair-like structures. These tiny hairs create grip through close contact with surfaces rather than glue or suction. This allows geckos to stick to glass, leaves, and even smooth ceilings. The grip is strong, yet the gecko can release it instantly by changing the angle of its toes. This makes climbing fast and effortless. Dirt does not ruin the grip because the pads clean themselves as the gecko walks. Using 67 rows of sticky pads turns almost any surface into a climbing path.

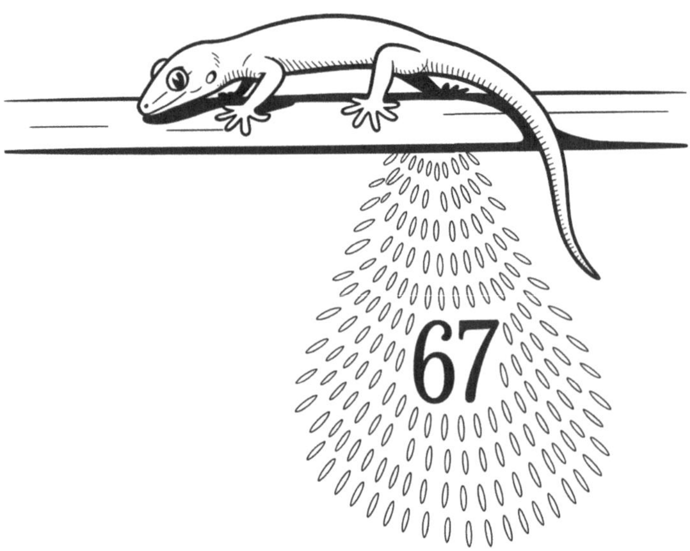

PLANETS

A WORLD WHERE GRAVITY FEELS 67 PERCENT STRONGER

Standing on **Jupiter** would make you feel **about 67 percent heavier** than you do on Earth.

Jupiter's enormous mass creates extremely strong gravity. Even though it is made mostly of gas, its size pulls objects inward with great force. This gravity helps hold dozens of moons in stable orbits and keeps Jupiter's thick atmosphere tightly bound. It also plays a role in protecting the inner solar system by pulling in or deflecting asteroids. Scientists study Jupiter's gravity to understand how giant planets influence everything around them. Feeling 67 percent heavier would make even simple movements exhausting.

67 MILLION MILES AWAY

Mars is, on average, **about 67 million miles away** from Earth.

This distance changes as both planets move around the Sun. Sometimes Mars is much closer, and other times it is far away on the opposite side of its orbit. The 67-million-mile average helps scientists plan space missions, calculate travel time, and communicate with spacecraft exploring the Red Planet.

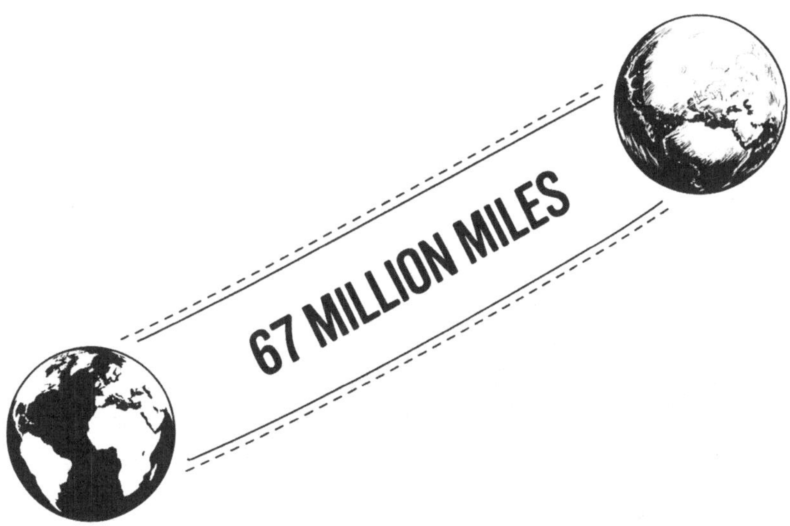

67 HOURS OF DARKNESS INSIDE A LUNAR CRATER

Some craters near the Moon's poles can remain dark for **up to 67 hours** without sunlight.

Because the Moon's axis is only slightly tilted, sunlight reaches polar regions at very low angles. Deep craters can stay in permanent shadow for long stretches of time. Temperatures inside these craters are extremely cold, cold enough to trap ice. Space missions have **detected frozen water hidden there**. These shadowed zones are important targets for future exploration. A 67-hour stretch of darkness creates some of the coldest places in the solar system.

67 RINGS OF WONDER

Saturn's ring system is made up of **at least 67 major ring sections and gaps.**

The rings are formed from countless pieces of ice and rock, ranging from tiny grains to objects as large as houses. Gaps appear where gravity from Saturn's moons pulls material away. Together, the rings and gaps create one of the most recognizable sights in the solar system.

67 DEGREES OF TILT

Unlike most planets that spin fairly upright, Uranus is tilted by **about 67 degrees**, causing it to roll through space almost on its side.

This extreme tilt makes Uranus's seasons very strange. For long periods of time, one pole points almost directly at the Sun while the other is left in darkness. As Uranus travels around the Sun, the roles slowly switch. Some parts of the planet experience decades of continuous sunlight, followed by decades of night. This unusual angle gives Uranus the **most extreme seasons of any planet** in our solar system.

67 PERCENT OF A PLANET HIDDEN BELOW CLOUDS

Nearly **67 percent of Venus's surface** is permanently hidden beneath thick clouds.

These clouds are so dense that **ordinary cameras cannot see through them.** They block visible light and reflect sunlight back into space. To study the surface, scientists use radar that can penetrate the clouds. This technology has revealed volcanoes, mountains, and vast plains below. Because the surface cannot cool easily, heat builds up over time. That **67 percent hidden world** makes Venus one of the hardest planets to study.

67 DAYS OF A MERCURIAN SEASON

A season on Mercury can last **about 67 days**, depending on where the planet is in its orbit.

Mercury spins slowly while racing around the Sun at high speed. This strange combination creates extreme temperature changes between day and night. During a single season, the planet's surface can swing from blistering heat to freezing cold, making Mercury one of the most extreme places in the solar system.

67 VOLCANOES ON ONE MOON

Jupiter's moon Io has **more than 67 active volcanoes**, making it the most volcanically active world in the solar system.

These volcanoes are powered by intense gravitational forces. As Io orbits Jupiter, the planet's gravity **squeezes and stretches** the moon, heating its interior. This constant flexing forces molten rock to erupt onto the surface. Some volcanic plumes on Io rise hundreds of kilometers into space, reshaping the moon again and again.

67 MILLION DEGREES AT THE SUN'S EDGE

The Sun's outer atmosphere, called the corona, can reach temperatures of **over 67 million degrees Fahrenheit.**

This is surprising because the **Sun's surface is much cooler than its atmosphere.** Scientists are still studying why the corona becomes so extremely hot. Powerful magnetic forces twist and snap above the Sun's surface, releasing huge amounts of energy. These explosions send heat and particles racing through space and can even affect Earth by creating auroras and disrupting satellites.

67 DAYS OF SPINNING STORMS

On some giant planets, enormous storms can spin and survive for **67 days or even longer** without breaking apart.

These storms are far bigger and stronger than anything on Earth. Gas giant planets have thick atmospheres filled with fast-moving winds that constantly feed energy into storms. Instead of fading away, the storms keep spinning, growing, and shifting as they pull heat from deep inside the planet. Some storms stretch wider than Earth itself and change shape slowly over time. Studying storms that last for 67 days helps scientists understand how weather behaves on planets with no solid surface at all.

SPINNING SIDEWAYS FOR 67 MILLION YEARS

Venus has likely been spinning in its unusual direction for **about 67 million years**.

Unlike most planets, Venus **rotates backward** compared to its orbit. Scientists believe this strange spin may have been caused by a massive collision long ago. Over time, the planet's thick atmosphere may have helped lock in this backward rotation. As a result, the Sun would appear to rise in the west and set in the east if you stood on Venus. One full day on Venus is longer than its year. That odd motion has remained stable for tens of millions of years.

67 YEARS TO KNOW A WORLD

Fully understanding a planet can take **around 67 years of study**, observation, and exploration.

Scientists begin with blurry telescope images and slowly gather more information over decades. Space missions may take years just to arrive, and each one collects only part of the story. New discoveries often raise more questions than answers. Over time, data from different missions are combined to map surfaces, measure gravity, and study atmospheres. Learning about a planet is a long process, and **67 years** can pass before scientists feel they truly understand a distant world.

67 YEARS

A PLANET THAT SPINS THROUGH A DAY IN 67 HOURS

A full day on **Neptune** lasts **about 67 Earth hours**, from one sunrise to the next.

Even though Neptune is enormous, it spins surprisingly fast. This rapid rotation helps power the strongest winds in the entire solar system. Clouds race across the planet at incredible speeds, circling the globe quickly. The fast spin also causes Neptune to bulge slightly around its middle. Scientists study this rotation to understand how energy moves inside gas giants. A 67-hour day keeps Neptune's atmosphere in constant motion. The planet never really gets a chance to calm down.

A FROZEN HIGHWAY STRETCHING 67 BILLION MILES

Beyond the last planet, space opens into a vast frozen region that stretches for **about 67 billion miles**.

This region is called the **Kuiper Belt**, and it is filled with icy worlds left over from the birth of the solar system. Temperatures here are so cold that gases like methane and nitrogen freeze solid. Pluto is one of the largest objects found in this distant zone, but thousands of smaller icy bodies are scattered throughout it. These objects rarely change because they are far from the Sun's heat. Scientists study the Kuiper Belt to learn how planets formed billions of years ago. Traveling across this 67-billion-mile stretch is like moving through a deep freezer of ancient space history.

67 MINUTES OF DEEP SPACE SILENCE

When spacecraft travel far from Earth, their radio signals can take **up to 67 minutes** to reach home.

This delay happens because radio waves travel at the speed of light, and **space is unimaginably vast**. During those 67 minutes, engineers on Earth cannot see what the spacecraft is doing or change its actions. Every movement must be planned in advance. The spacecraft must think for itself, using onboard computers to make decisions. This long silence shows just how far human technology has reached into the solar system.

A FAMILIAR VISITOR THAT RETURNS EVERY 67 YEARS

Halley's Comet becomes visible from Earth roughly **once every 67 years**.

This comet follows a long, stretched orbit that carries it far beyond the outer planets before pulling it back toward the Sun. When Halley's Comet approaches the inner solar system, heat causes its icy surface to release gas and dust, forming a glowing head and a long tail that can stretch millions of miles. Ancient astronomers recorded its appearances thousands of years ago, long before comets were understood. Each return looks slightly different as the comet slowly loses material. For many people, seeing Halley's Comet is a **once-in-a-lifetime experience**. Its 67-year journey links generations of skywatchers across history.

DINOSAURS

67 FEET FROM HEAD TO TAIL

Some of the largest dinosaurs could stretch **up to 67 feet long**, making them longer than most houses.

These enormous dinosaurs were often long-necked plant eaters that spent much of their day feeding. Their extended necks allowed them to reach leaves high in trees without needing to move constantly, saving energy. The long tail played an important role as well, helping balance their massive bodies while walking. Being 67 feet long also **offered protection**, as very few predators could challenge an animal of that size. Fossils of dinosaurs this long help scientists understand how bones, muscles, and joints worked together to support such gigantic bodies.

WEARING A SHIELD FOR 67 MILLION YEARS

Euoplocephalus survived for **around 67 million years** by relying on armor instead of speed.

Its body was covered in thick, bony plates that acted like a built-in shield. These plates protected its back, sides, and even parts of its head from sharp teeth and claws. The dinosaur stayed low to the ground, making it difficult for predators to flip it over. If attacked, Euoplocephalus could also swing its heavy tail club to strike with force. This combination of armor and defense meant it did not need to run away. Over millions of years, this slow but **steady strategy** proved highly successful. Being hard to injure helped Euoplocephalus survive in a dangerous world.

CARRYING THE WEIGHT OF 67 TONS

Some of the heaviest dinosaurs may have weighed **as much as 67 tons**, making them among the largest land animals to ever exist.

Supporting this much weight required incredibly strong bones and thick, powerful muscles. Their **legs acted like massive pillars**, spreading the load evenly as they moved. These dinosaurs likely moved slowly, carefully placing each step to avoid injury. Their size affected the environment around them, flattening plants and shaping the landscape as they traveled. Studying dinosaurs that reached 67 tons helps scientists learn how living creatures can grow so large without collapsing under their own weight.

FISHING LIKE A PRO FOR 67 MILLION YEARS

Spinosaurus survived for **about 67 million years** by hunting fish instead of chasing land animals.

This dinosaur lived near rivers, lakes, and swamps, where fish were plentiful. Its long, narrow snout was filled with smooth, cone-shaped teeth that were perfect for gripping slippery prey. Unlike sharp slicing teeth, these teeth prevented fish from wriggling free. Strong arms helped scoop prey from the water, and its tail was built for swimming rather than fast running. Scientists believe Spinosaurus spent much of its time in or near water, avoiding competition with other meat-eaters. Its tall sail may have helped regulate body temperature or signal to others. Fishing for millions of years made Spinosaurus one of the most unusual predators of its time.

BUILT TO CHEW ALL DAY WITH 67 TEETH

Some plant-eating dinosaurs used **around 67 teeth at a time** to grind tough prehistoric plants.

These teeth were packed tightly together and worked like natural grinding tools. As leaves and branches wore the teeth down, new ones grew in to replace them. This constant replacement allowed dinosaurs to **eat nonstop**, which was necessary to fuel their enormous bodies. Fossilized teeth help scientists learn what dinosaurs ate and how ancient plant life shaped their survival.

LIVING UNDERGROUND FOR 67 SAFE DAYS

Oryctodromeus may have **stayed hidden** in underground burrows for **about 67 days** at a time.

Fossils of this small dinosaur have been found inside tunnel-like structures, suggesting it could dig and live below the surface. Burrows **offered protection** from large predators that could not fit inside. They also helped shield the dinosaur from extreme heat, cold, and storms. Young dinosaurs could grow safely inside these underground spaces. Strong arms helped with digging, while a stiff tail provided balance in tight tunnels. Spending weeks underground made Oryctodromeus one of the few dinosaurs adapted for a hidden lifestyle.

WALKING LIKE EARTHSHAKERS AT 67 TONS

When dinosaurs weighing **up to 67 tons** walked across soft ground, their footsteps could leave deep impressions that sometimes turned into fossils.

These footprints reveal how weight was distributed across their feet and how slowly and carefully they moved. Some fossilized tracks show dinosaurs traveling in groups, suggesting social behavior. A single 67-ton step could press layers of mud into shapes that survived for millions of years, giving scientists direct evidence of how these giants moved.

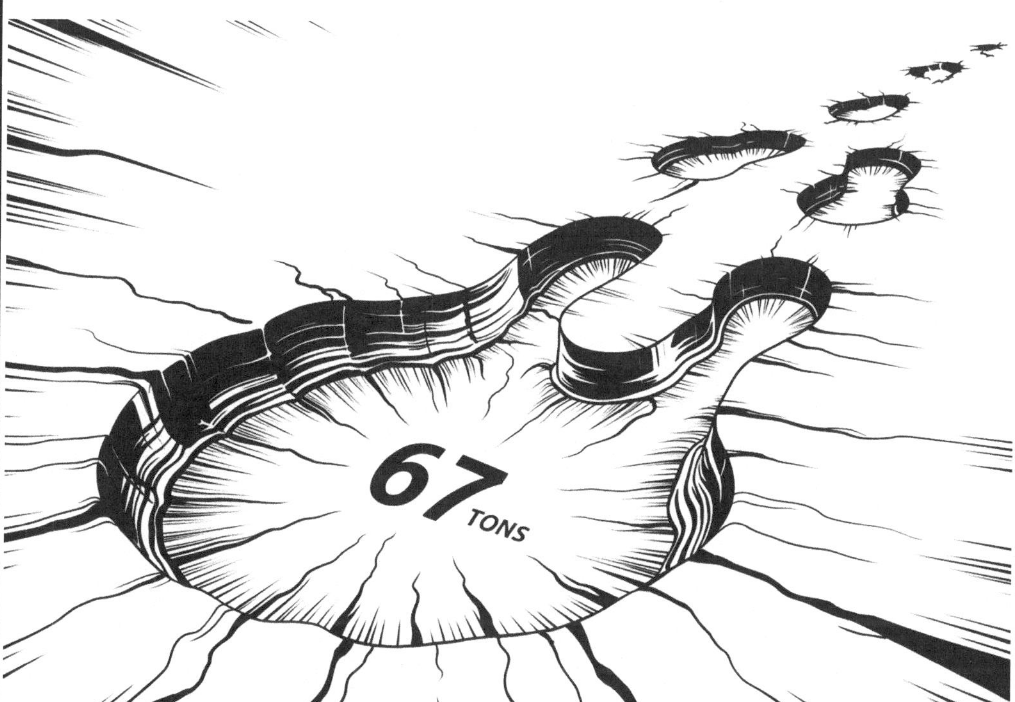

A HEAD BUILT FOR 67 POWERFUL HEADBUTTS

A **Pachycephalosaurus** had a thick, rounded skull built to handle **up to 67 strong impacts**.

The dome on top of its head was made of dense bone, far thicker than that of most dinosaurs. This structure helped protect the brain during collisions. Scientists think Pachycephalosaurus may have used its head to push, shove, or ram rivals during contests. Strong neck muscles absorbed shock and helped control movement. These headbutts were likely used to compete for territory or mates rather than for fighting predators. Fossil skulls show signs of repeated stress, suggesting this behavior happened often. With a head designed for impact, Pachycephalosaurus was built to win pushing contests.

67 MILLION YEARS LOCKED IN STONE

Long after dinosaurs vanished, their bones lay hidden underground for **about 67 million years**, waiting in complete silence.

When a dinosaur died, its body could be quickly buried by mud, sand, or ash. Over time, heavy layers pressed down, and mineral-rich water slowly flowed through the bones. Bit by bit, the minerals replaced the bone material, **turning it into stone**. This transformation happened so slowly that it took millions of years to complete.

During those 67 million years, oceans moved, continents drifted, and entire landscapes changed above the fossils. No one knew the dinosaurs were there until wind, rain, and time revealed them again. Every fossil uncovered today is a piece of deep history, preserved through an unimaginable stretch of time beneath the Earth's surface.

A ROAR THAT COULD TRAVEL 67 METERS

Some large dinosaurs may have produced sounds that carried **up to 67 meters** across forests and open land.

Instead of loud, sharp roars like those in movies, many dinosaurs likely made **deep, low-frequency calls**. These sounds travel farther and lose less energy as they move through trees and uneven terrain. Dinosaurs may have used these calls to warn rivals, attract mates, or keep track of others in their group. Fossil skull shapes and comparisons with modern animals like crocodiles and birds help scientists estimate how far these sounds could travel. A call reaching 67 meters would have allowed dinosaurs to **communicate without needing to see one another**.

SEEING CLEARLY IN 67 PERCENT LOW LIGHT

A **Tyrannosaurus rex** could see well in **about 67 percent lower light** than humans.

Large eye sockets suggest excellent night and dawn vision. This helped T. rex hunt during low-light hours when prey was less alert. Its forward-facing eyes provided strong depth perception for targeting. Combined with smell and hearing, vision made it a powerful predator. Seeing clearly in dim light gave T. rex a major advantage.

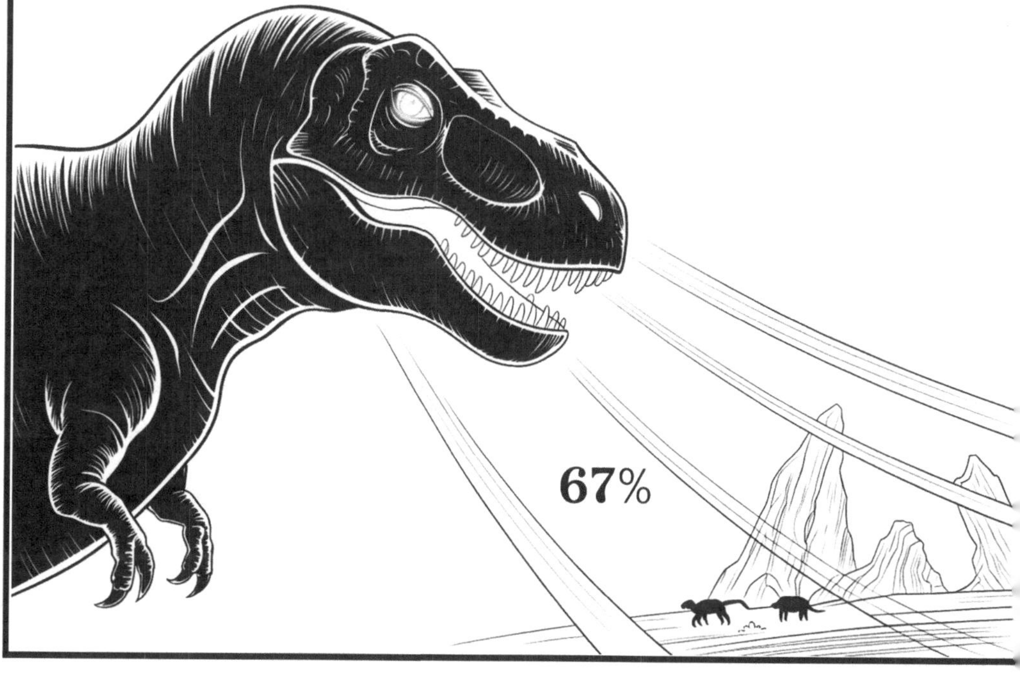

ONLY 67 GRAMS TO CONTROL A GIANT

Despite their massive size, some large dinosaurs had brains weighing **only about 67 grams**.

Brain size alone does not determine intelligence. Dinosaurs relied heavily on instinct, sharp senses, and learned behavior rather than complex thinking. Their nervous systems were well suited for balance, movement, and survival tasks. Fossil skulls allow scientists to estimate brain size and structure. A 67-gram brain was enough to control a body weighing many tons, showing that dinosaurs were **efficient thinkers** built for survival, not problem-solving.

SLEEPING THROUGH DANGER FOR 67 MINUTES AT A TIME

Some dinosaurs may have rested in short bursts lasting **around 67 minutes**, instead of sleeping for long stretches.

Living in a world full of predators meant staying alert was important. Rather than deep sleep, dinosaurs may have rested lightly, waking often to scan their surroundings. Fossil evidence and comparisons with modern reptiles and birds suggest that **short rest cycles helped dinosaurs recover energy** while still staying aware of danger. Sleeping in shorter blocks also allowed herds to take turns watching for threats, increasing the group's chances of survival.

HOW LONG COULD A DINOSAUR HOLD ITS BREATH? 67 SECONDS

Some dinosaurs may have been able to hold their breath for **up to 67 seconds** when they needed to.

Many dinosaurs likely had lungs that worked more like those of modern birds than humans. This type of lung system moves air through the body in one direction, making breathing more efficient. Because of this, dinosaurs may have been able to pause their breathing for short periods without harm. Holding their breath for around 67 seconds could have helped them cross rivers, walk through dusty areas, or stay calm during sudden danger. Even a small ability like this could make survival easier in a busy prehistoric world.

PROTECTING A NEST FOR 67 STRAIGHT DAYS

An Oviraptor likely stayed close to its nest for **around 67 days** while its eggs developed.

Fossils of Oviraptor have been found sitting directly on top of nests, with arms spread protectively over the eggs. This position is very similar to how modern birds brood their eggs. Remaining at the nest for such a long time meant the adult had to defend against predators, harsh weather, and hunger. Staying still also helped keep the eggs at a steady temperature, which is important for healthy development. The parent may have taken short breaks to feed but always returned quickly. Guarding a nest for 67 days shows that some dinosaurs were not just egg layers, but devoted parents.

TRAVELING TOGETHER FOR 67 MILES

Some dinosaurs may have traveled **up to 67 miles together** as a group while searching for food and water.

Fossil trackways show long lines of footprints heading in the same direction, often made by dinosaurs of different sizes. This suggests adults and young moved together as a herd. Traveling long distances helped dinosaurs reach fresh plants and avoid areas where food had run out. Moving as a group also **offered protection**, since predators were less likely to attack many dinosaurs at once. A 67-mile journey would have taken time and coordination, showing that these dinosaurs were **strong travelers and careful planners**.

TRIVIA

FIND THE DIFFER ENCES

CAN YOU SPOT 5 DIFFERENCES IN EACH IMAGE?

67

67

6
7

6
7

67

67

67
SALON

67

MAZE PUZZLES

LEVEL: EASY

LEVEL: EASY

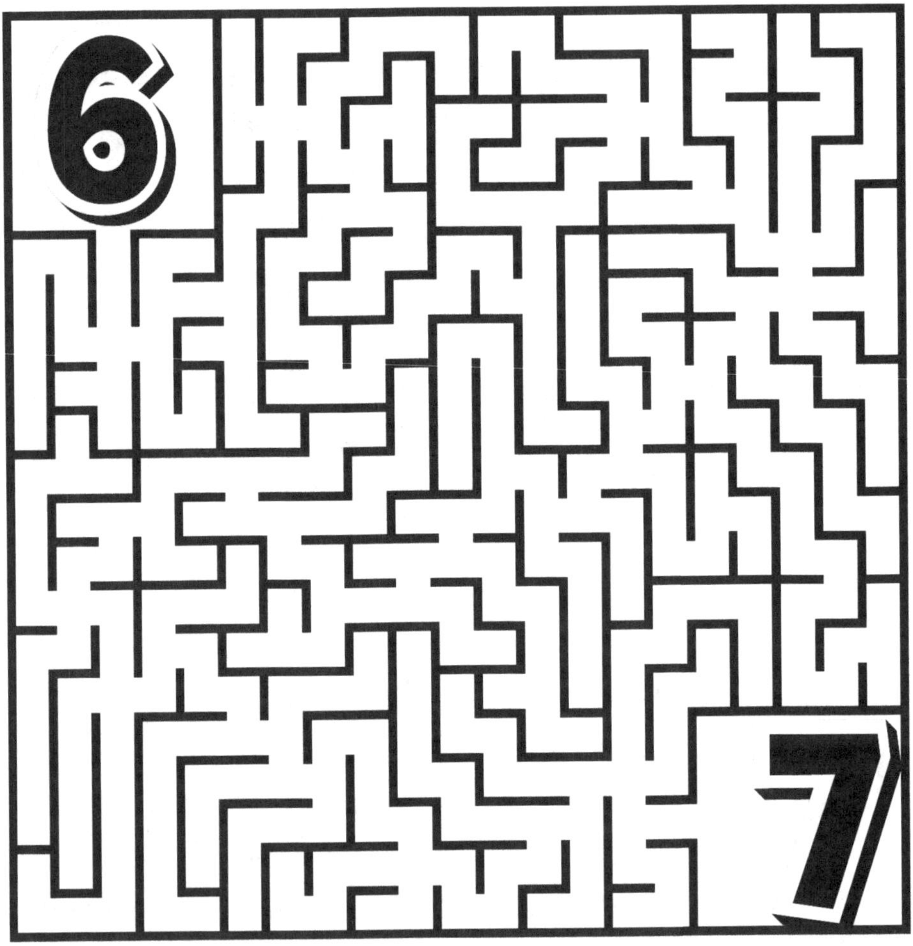

LEVEL: MEDIUM

LEVEL: HARD

67

LEVEL: HARD

WORD SCRAMBLE

THE ULTIMATE
MEME SCRAMBLE

Unscramble the following words

SMEEM ____________________

MSARCS ____________________

UYNOG HTGU ____________________

ALRTEABEL ____________________

IRALV ____________________

DEABS ____________________

PUOLWG ____________________

ZIRZ ____________________

IMAGS ____________________

EYET ____________________

ON PAC ____________________

LGRIAOHMT ____________________

SONCEERHAT ______________________

AKDN ______________________

PIOUMC ______________________

LEXF ______________________

TECSIAETH ______________________

VBSEI ______________________

TANS ______________________

CAECENLLD ______________________

EEPRFMLOTAD ______________________

LORTL ______________________

BACKTILIC ______________________

MODFNA ______________________

SATHCIF ______________________

MTONEMC NCTSEIO ______________________

ODBLECK ____________________

AOWDBSHAN ____________________

ESTERLIVAM ____________________

ETEMAPLT ____________________

MOIEJ REOC ____________________

SOLEMEHW ____________________

DNRET ____________________

RETLIF ____________________

INAM CARCARETH ____________________

RIPEDEFED EEMM ____________________

ERENG LGAF ____________________

RSCOL ____________________

LITHUMNAB ____________________

CKILC ____________________

YOEBKADR IORWRAR ______________________

TNENIRET EFEB ______________________

EMEP GPAE ______________________

NIESID KEOJ ______________________

SYSSA ______________________

NUFLEORICN ______________________

IBVE HKECC ______________________

TFI HECCK ______________________

XELFGIN ______________________

UQENE NYGEER ______________________

TRAXE ______________________

CPAL CBAK ______________________

RITGERGS ______________________

SIRTTHY ______________________

ANSWERS

MEMES

SARCASM

YOUNG THUG

RELATABLE

VIRAL

BASED

GLOWUP

RIZZ

SIGMA

YEET

NO CAP

ALGORITHM

SCREENSHOT

DANK

COPIUM

FLEX

AESTHETIC

VIBES

STAN

CANCELLED

DEPLATFORM

TROLL

CLICKBAIT

FANDOM

CATFISH

COMMENT SECTION

BLOCKED

SHADOWBAN

LIVESTREAM

TEMPLATE

EMOJI CORE

WHOLESOME

TREND

FILTER

MAIN CHARACTER

DEEPFRIED MEME

GREEN FLAG

SCROLL

THUMBNAIL

CLICK

MEME GAME

KEYBOARD WARRIOR

INSIDE JOKE

SASSY

INFLUENCER

VIBE CHECK

FIT CHECK

FLEXING

QUEEN ENERGY

EXTRA

CLAP BACK

TRIGGERS

THIRSTY

INTERNET BEEF

CERTIFICATE OF CURIOSITY

THIS CERTIFIES THAT

HAS EXPLORED 67 FUN AND FASCINATING FACTS ABOUT ANIMALS, PLANETS, DINOSAURS, AND WEIRD SCIENCE.

DATE:

67